THE CHURCH NEEDS THE LAITY

THE CHURCH NEEDS THE LAITY

The Wisdom of JOHN HENRY NEWMAN

MICHAEL W. HIGGINS

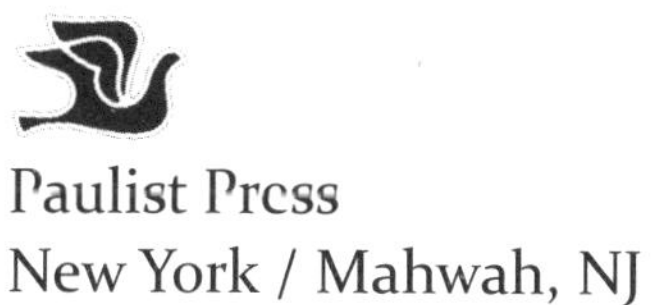

Paulist Press
New York / Mahwah, NJ

Published by Paulist Press
997 Macarthur Boulevard
Mahwah, New Jersey 07430
www.paulistpress.com

Cover image (background) by HorenkO/Shutterstock.com
Cover and book design by Lynn Else

Copyright © 2021 by Michael W. Higgins

All rights reserved. No part of this publication may be reproduced, stored in a retrieval system, or transmitted in any form or by any means, electronic, mechanical, photocopying, recording, scanning, or otherwise, without either the prior written permission of the Publisher, or authorization through payment of the appropriate per-copy fee to the Copyright Clearance Center, Inc., www.copyright.com. Requests to the Publisher for permission should be addressed to the Permissions Department, Paulist Press, permissions@paulistpress.com.

Library of Congress Cataloging-in-Publication Data
Names: Higgins, Michael W., author.
Title: The church needs the laity : the wisdom of John Henry Newman / Michael W. Higgins.
Description: New York / Mahwah, NJ : Paulist Press, 2021. | Summary: "A conversational discussion of the impact of John Henry Newman on Catholic thought, especially where it concerns the importance and involvement of the laity in all facets of the church, including the formulation of what we believe"—Provided by publisher.
Identifiers: LCCN 2020023080 (print) | LCCN 2020023081 (ebook) | ISBN 9780809155217 (paperback) | ISBN 9781587689161 (ebook)
Subjects: LCSH: Newman, John Henry, 1801-1890. | Laity. | Catholic Church—Doctrines.
Classification: LCC BX4705.N5 H54 2021 (print) | LCC BX4705.N5 (ebook) | DDC 262/.152—dc23
LC record available at https://lccn.loc.gov/2020023080
LC ebook record available at https://lccn.loc.gov/2020023081

ISBN 978-0-8091-5521-7 (paperback)
ISBN 978-1-58768-916-1 (e-book)

Published in Canada by Novalis
Publishing Office
1 Eglinton Avenue East, Suite 800
Toronto, Ontario, Canada
M4P 3A1

Head Office
4475 Frontenac Street
Montréal, Québec, Canada
H2H 2S2
www.novalis.ca

Cataloguing in Publication is available from Library and Archives Canada.
ISBN: 978-2-89688-868-9

We acknowledge the support of the Government of Canada.

Printed and bound in the
United States of America

To the women in my family—Krystyna, Becca, Sarah, and Alexa—who keep my still-ingrained clericalist impulses in check and to whom I am forever indebted

CONTENTS

FOREWORD

Michael W. Higgins, Distinguished Professor Emeritus of Catholic Thought at Sacred Heart University, is well-known as a leading voice in the conversation about Catholic higher education. In this work he invites us into his own intellectual journey, a journey in which John Henry Newman is both a theme for Higgins's scholarly work as a professor and a trusted companion as Higgins serves as department chair, dean, college president, and vice chancellor.

I first met Newman as a fledgling theology scholar. Impatient with the church, I took solace in his critique of the clergy and thoughtful support for the individual conscience. Decades later, working with junior faculty new to the culture of a Catholic university, I found these insights by Newman were a useful shorthand, signaling to sceptics that a Catholic institution by its very nature would value intellectual freedom.

Higgins wants much more. His agenda is ambitious, seeking to revitalize Catholic public discourse in all its depth and beauty and capacity for novelty. Seared by the ramifications of the sexual abuse crisis on the institution he loves, he has spoken clearly, early, and often about the need for church reform and for a vigorous role for the laity in that process. This is not a new theme, Higgins insists; there have been several points in history in which the church was stabilized—and rerouted—due to the efforts of a "resilient," "steadfast" laity in the face of a "fractious," "weak," and "intransigent" clergy.

But it is Newman who has been his guide in this effort; indeed, it is Newman's own "turn to the laity"—as rector, inviting lay leadership for the university college in Dublin—that is the decisive model. In Newman, Higgins finds a champion of "university culture"—a phrase that sounds almost strange today, one that emphasizes rigor and independent thinking, and one that firmly rejects the reduction of that culture to utilitarian or pragmatic ends (including, in Higgins's term, a "creeping managerialism"). The same is true of our political culture, he claims, which explains Higgins's further call for the emergence of a culture of public conversation among Catholic intellectuals—presumably, to nurture those laypersons who will emerge to lead in the church and in Catholic higher education.

For Higgins, it is Newman who foresaw the means and goals of such a culture: "He knew that truth emerges out of the collision of intellects, that communion defeats sectarianism, that the imagination can be a vehicle of grace, that spiritual companionship is more than succor: it is life-generating for the mind and for the heart."

We will need every one of those bracing words. I write at a moment of profound disruption, as the COVID-19 pandemic has led to a widespread health and economic crisis. With most of the country, we are staying home, emerging only for necessities, and large swaths of the economy are idled. I teach my university courses online, moving from cutting vegetables in the kitchen to the demanding screen in the tiny back bedroom and then, to clear my head, to the living room to add one more piece to the unfinished puzzle on the battered coffee table. And back to the demanding screen.

There is no "going to Mass" now; the churches are closed to the public. We watch the sacraments, huddled in our homes, scanning the internet. The news media portrays the institutional church in the figure of the pope, now alone in the cavernous Vatican, reaching out—*urbi et orbi*—with ancient texts interleaved with pleas for compassion, service, and solidarity. On Good Friday, St. Peter's Square was empty, a small band of carefully spaced votaries walked in the dark, lit by torches marking the Stations of the Cross.

Asked about the laity, Newman famously observed, Higgins reminds us "that the church would look foolish without them." I don't know that anyone ever imagined putting this scenario into action, but here we are: The Triduum was televised. And the laity disappeared. Reduced to the "essentials," as safety required a limited cast, the live-streamed liturgies we saw were often the work of a single presider and deacon, perhaps with a cantor off-screen. The responding church was at home, attending in posture and prayer or watching reverently or listening on headphones while driving a delivery van. When my own university puts out marketing videos, it says it is "socializing" the experience. This experience did not seem "social" to me. I was watching TV.

In this extraordinary situation, was Newman right? Yes and no. The clergy do not look foolish; they are simply trying to serve. But the sacraments on the screen seem very far away, in a closed circle of action. The professionally produced visuals from the Vatican and the larger cathedrals are astonishing in their beauty, the presiders sure in the ritual language and searching in the homilies. Live streams from local parishes are less sophisticated, but their value is clear as they connect a parish community with a familiar pastoral presence. The clergy do not look foolish—but I do, singing the great amen to a pixilated screen, to a sacramental moment that does not register my voice.

Higgins would urge me to look again. Newman's gift to his own age was a very Catholic "attention to the secular": nothing is foreign to this gospel, and novelty is to be weighed on its own terms. As I struggled, with my university colleagues, to shift my teaching from a classroom environment to a variety of online platforms, it was bracing to find Higgins already ahead of me in this area as well, suggesting that this "digital age" opens the way for a pedagogical model of the faculty member as "guide and mentor"—and even that this model more closely resembles the "particular genius of the medieval university." For my own impatience with the live-stream Mass, Higgins would push for a broad rethinking of eucharistic participation as well, one that not merely rejects the novelty but pushes into it, to find a new Catholic frame.

As befits an introduction to Newman, these pages are crafted with an eye to the formation of mind and heart. In this Higgins offers the reader a model of the serious engagement he enjoins, and a permission to think clearly and rigorously about the Catholic tradition and the dimensions of our own day. In a time of transition, Higgins's claim that Newman saw the task of theology to be "accustoming the mind of Catholics to the idea of change" seems arrestingly fresh and, dare I say, hopeful. As Catholic colleges and universities consider their mission going forward, they would be well served to let this thoughtful introduction to Newman shape the sensibility with which they will face the necessary decisions to come.

May Blessed John Henry Newman lead the way. We are grateful that Michael Higgins is here to rally us in his wake, to hold the lantern high.

Nancy Dallavalle
Holy Saturday, April 11, 2020

PREFACE

It is hard to imagine that the gates of hell will prevail against it. We have assurances, Catholics will argue, from no less an authority than the Gospels, that Christ's church will never be destroyed, its enemies never in the end triumphant. But what if the enemies are from within? What if the sundering of the communion of the faithful is an inside job? What if?

Again and again we are hit by wave after wave—an unending tsunami that offers little respite for recovery—of scandals: clerical sex abuse, episcopal coverup, head office financial skullduggery (not limited to the Vatican), the toppling of revered religious and spiritual leaders whose peccadilloes are writ large, along with a score of theological and moral dustups that leave the committed confused, outsiders mystified, and detractors gleeful.

It's all an unholy mess. Church historian Massimo Faggioli and former Dominican Master General and spiritual writer Timothy Ratcliffe are just two well-known and respected Catholic figures who judge the current clerical sex abuse crisis the greatest challenge to Catholic credibility since the Reformation. Christiane Amanpour, the international news media celebrity, has warned that the Catholic Church faces unrelenting decline as a consequence of failing to get its act together, and the Jesuit president of the Gregorian University's Centre for Child Protection, Hans Zollner, has, with unmassaged Teutonic bluntness, declared that the sex abuse scandals could destroy the church as an institution.

Enter John Henry Cardinal Newman—newly minted saint and Victorian polymath.

Newman is no solo saviour. When we invest heavily in the charisma of our exemplars, models, and leaders, we leave ourselves open to grave disappointment when they don't deliver. But Newman provides—in his writings and in his life—an estimable figure of personal integrity, intellectual rigour, and honest character. You knew where you stood with Newman in the end, although he could be elusive, oblique, and calculating at times, and you knew that you could trust his insights because they were tested in fire.

Newman championed the laity when the church barely recognized their existence; he established their importance by demonstrating that the lay voice had saved the church when its ordained went off the rails; he recovered what had been lost or suppressed for centuries.

If the church *qua* institution is existentially imperiled as Zollner and others argue, then it may well be another historical instance when the laity saves the church. A *kairos* moment.

What follows is *not* a manifesto or an ecclesial *J'accuse*, even less a *tuba mirum*. It is but one effort to rally believers around the reclamation of the lay charism as the corrective to the sin of clericalism—as it has been dubbed by prelates and prophets alike—by drawing on the wisdom and witness of Newman. Others too have written about the laity—distinguished ecclesiologists like Yves Congar and Paul Lakeland to name but two—but Newman's work is where it started for Catholic Christianity, and in keeping with his own injunction to go to the sources, I have gone right back to Newman.

This essay wouldn't exist were it not for the invitation from Donna Crilly, senior academic editor at Paulist Press, following an address to Catholic publishers in Chicago that I gave in the late summer of 2019. The time and the topic formed a convenient marriage. Now to make something of it.

Some of the material in this short volume was drawn from some previous work I did on Newman: "John Henry Newman: A Century of Influence," *Grail* 7, no. 3 (1991); "John Henry Newman: The Way of Catholic Education," in *The Philosophy of Catholic Education*, edited by Caroline DiGiovanni (Toronto: Novalis, 1992); "The Cardinal and the Monk: Literary and Theological Convergences in Newman and Merton," *The Merton Annual* 5 (1992). The personal recollections are designed to situate this memoir/essay within the broader challenges facing intellectual leadership in our and not an earlier time. But they are connected, and Newman is the *pontifex*.

We are what our history and our context make us: the colleagues with whom we work; the mentors who inspire and shape us; the friends who correct our excess. I have been especially privileged to study under James M. Cameron (not the *Titanic* guy); to work with Douglas R. Letson, president emeritus of St. Jerome's University in the University of Waterloo, Ontario, Canada, my coauthor for some five books and the person I succeeded as the second lay president of St. Jerome's; and to befriend and to cooperate with John Petillo, president of Sacred Heart University, Fairfield, Connecticut, in the making of a Catholic university slightly outside the norm, a pioneer for a new era of North American Catholic higher education.

There are many books on John Henry Newman—Victorian churchman, *belle-lettrist*, correspondent and diarist extraordinaire (even by nineteenth-century standards), occasional novelist, poet and hymnologist, patristics scholar, theological luminary, university leader and educationist, and a spiritual and devotional writer of popular appeal—that we really don't need another. Even now, when this very English cardinal has been raised to the altars, his cred and relevance never greater, his ecumenical impact continues unfolding in surprising quarters.

Still, in the face of such daunting realities, I think there is a continuing space for a personal essay on the significance of the life and thought of this Catholic giant on contemporary folk. On people like me.

And so what follows is an undertaking that combines the personal voice with a scrutiny of the legacy, my effort to place Newman within the context of the challenges facing the Catholic public intellectual by sifting him through an autobiographical lens. I don't think he would mind. After all, he is known for his gift for autobiography, his *Apologia pro Vita Sua* a classic of the genre.

Studies of Newman will continue to proliferate, his work the subject of countless dissertations and theses in countless languages and disciplines. And there is need for primers and brief histories acquainting emerging generations with the jewels to be mined in the Newman industry. English historian Eamon Duffy's *John Henry Newman: A Very Brief History* serves this need with his customary eloquence and concision. In his introduction he nicely encapsulates the reasons why contemporary Catholic progressives find Newman's attractiveness as an intellectual and Catholic irresistible:

> As a Catholic, he rejected doctrinaire demands for unquestioning obedience to contemporary church formulae as if they were timeless truths. In an authoritarian church he was an ardent defender of the legitimate autonomy of the theologian, and, in a clericalist age, insisted on the role of the laity as custodians and not mere recipients of the faith of the Church.[1]

These are the reasons why I have been Newman-bound for most of my life as a student and professor. He spoke to me *out* of his time and *into* my time; he seduced me with his magisterial command of language and concept; he inspired me with his transdisciplinarity—a common feature to be found in the thinkers of his era unfazed by our contemporary obsession with expertise, knowledge stratification, silos of competence, unassailable oracles of authority within straightening bonds of scholarly credibility.

He knew how to stretch the mind, and he knew how to do it elegantly.

This essay, then—personal, laced with autobiography, a mix of probing and cautious reflection—is rooted in a specific time, place, and professional trajectory. He is Newman as I discovered him. A Newman of the text, for sure, a Newman mediated by memoir, volume, and tract, a Newman that fit comfortably in the curricula of undergraduate and graduate courses in English literature, a Newman whose portrait and name graced chapels and study rooms in the premier secular universities, a Newman whose conversion to Catholicism was a defining moment for church life and teaching.

That Newman, and more besides.

I

MY JOURNEY WITH NEWMAN

This is how I came to him.

I had studied a small section of the *Apologia* in high school—a public secondary in downtown Toronto that was mostly Jewish in its constitution—and I knew him only as a convert and Catholic. I was tribally proud. Good for our side.

And then he went largely unnoticed as I worked my way through my baccalaureate and master's degrees, only to resurface with an unnerving potency as I began my doctoral studies as a Victorianist at Toronto's York University.

Schooled in the vast tomes of John Ruskin, the poetry of the pre-Raphaelites, the mighty volumes of verse in the Tennyson and Browning canons, the complex and intricate genius of both the minor and major figures of the *fin-de-siècle*—I had earlier in my university career written a thesis on that most peculiar of eccentric Catholic writers, Frederick William Serafino Austin Lewis Mary Rolfe (Baron Corvo)—I was nicely poised for a life of scholarship in post-Romantic English literature. Thomas Merton would come along at some point and propel me in another direction entirely—giving up *Praeterita* for *The Seven Storey Mountain* in the process. But that is another story.

While in the penultimate year of my PhD coursework, I was encouraged to take a class in theology at our sister and senior university, the University of Toronto, under the direction of Professor James M. Cameron. University professor in three disciplines—philosophy, English, and theology—Cameron had a unique status that positioned him nicely for the final years of his life as a teacher and public intellectual. Previously, he had been chair of philosophy at Leeds University and master of Rutherford College, University of Kent (Canterbury)—before he was lured this side of the Atlantic. Situated at the University of St. Michael's College—the Catholic federated university in the constituent University of Toronto—students, undergraduate and graduate, across the large university campus had access to him. Through the joint doctoral program in Victorian studies between the U of T and York, I too would have access to him.

His course—"Tractarianism and Its Influence Upon Anglican Theology"—was your then-conventional twenty-six-week arrangement, and the experience proved the most demanding, focused, and enlightening of all my doctoral work. And long-lasting in its effect.

For sure, it was about Anglicanism, but it was primarily about Newman and his formative role in the shaping of the Oxford Movement, the crafting and dissemination of the movement's controversial tracts—monographs promoting a particular position of consequence for the revival of the Catholic dimension of the *ecclesia anglicana*—as well as being about Newman's subsequent disquiet over his earlier theological and historical positions as he came, reluctantly but inexorably, to reassess his very relationship to the church that ordained him, the church that he loved, the Church of England, his grand *via media*. I learned a great deal about the renascence of an apostolic and patristic infusion in the life of the established church, but I learned much more about Newman, his Anglican life and his Roman life, his masterworks, his rich interaction with his age, his devotion to his disciples and his sometimes anguished sense of responsibility for them, and his perplexingly fraught relationship with the authorities in Rome.

He was a man who was both loved and distrusted by the church of his birth and the church he adopted; he was a man deeply admired by his peers and yet accused of the most unsavory of motives. And, withal, he was a person of unflinching intellectual integrity, though maligned and traduced for decades.

What I learned from Cameron's tutorials—the class was conducted in the Oxbridge manner, as he was a graduate of Balliol College and a keen supporter of its pedagogical paradigm—was more, far more, than a dissection of the text, biweekly papers, and extensive reading of primary sources. What Cameron embodied was the Newman *approach* to the life of the mind; he lived what Newman thought essential to the right flourishing of the human capacity to know, to search. Cameron attached high importance to the *public* component of the shaping of young minds; he insisted that as students and as intellectuals-in-the-making we had an obligation to engage with society, eschew the easy comforts of scholarly cloistering, opt for lucidity and logic over academic obfuscation and imaginative whimsy, keep language luminous—opacity and parasense his *bête noir*. Parasense, Cameron argued in his published lectures delivered on the occasion of the 150th anniversary of the founding of the University of Toronto and 125th anniversary of the founding of St. Michael's College, differs

> from what may be taken as nonsense, in that there are no category blunders and no obvious logical foul-ups. It seems grammatical; its words are for the most part to be found in the established dictionaries; the syntax conforms to standard models and thus our habitual expectations are fulfilled; above all, it is as though it were coated with a special kind of grease—it slips down (or past) easily. It may even be redeemable in a curious way: as being code.... Commonly, though, such a piece of parasense is chosen because it generates intellectual fog and induces a reverential attitude in the reader. It is like the chanting of a *mantra* or spell, except that a *mantra* may make beautiful sense for one who understands the religious discourse within which it is uttered.[1]

What teacher or reader has not come across instances of parasense in both their professional and personal lives? Impenetrable jargon disguised as erudition? Mock profundity dressed up in the argot of officialese? Dense writing that purports to be sagacious when in fact it is risible?

Ministry of Education reports, academic studies, political commission summaries, and ecclesiastical briefs are all prey to the intellectual infection of parasense. The only way to cure or arrest the contagion, in Cameron's view, is to cultivate the intellectual habit of thinking clearly, writing clearly, communicating clearly. This does not mean bereft of style or the appealing qualities to be found in the unique voice that stretches conventional usage and form; what it does mean, irrespective the mode of delivery, is that one says what one wants to say in ways that respect comprehension rather than dazzle with befuddlement.

Just think of Frau Grubach in Franz Kafka's *The Trial*, Josef K's landlady, who believes the mysterious investigators who come to her house, because they must be profound, as she didn't understand a thing they were saying. She didn't understand because it was all inane circularity of argument, vacuous, meaningless. We are so easily duped by sophistical wordsmiths that only a clear-headed attentiveness to words and how their meaning is mangled can ensure, can guarantee, our freedom. The wild rhetoric of populist politicians is ample contemporary evidence of how the corruption of speech imperils democratic governance, the rights and freedoms of citizens, usurping in the process all foundations for trust, shared meaning, the working presumption of objective truth, the bonds that cement communities.

Cameron urged his students to engage constantly with the communities—political, social, academic, and ecclesial—in which they lived, and he did so by modeling the ideal of the public intellectual in his own work and in his own life: speaking to parish groups; writing letters to the editor in newspapers and magazines (Catholic and non-Catholic); contributing regularly to the *New York Review of Books*, the *Tablet*, and *Commonweal*; publishing essays (his preferred genre) in peer-reviewed journals; and giving public lectures at universities, including prestigious series at Yale and the University of Notre Dame.

It was because of Cameron that I have attempted in my own career as an academic, as a radio documentarian for the Canadian Broadcasting Corporation, and as writer and biographer to speak to, and write for, diverse audiences without condescension, or, as we would now say, without dumbing down, valuing the efficacy of the right word, seeking to enlighten and not to befuddle, exercising a ministry of truth in a climate that often privileges inventive prevarication—entertaining but lethal.

In teaching me Newman he provided, whether he knew it or not, an exemplar of the fiercely critical and fearlessly faithful catholic public intellectual and scholar.

What the eminent Newman editor and fellow Oratorian Charles Stephen Dessain says of Newman I can say of Cameron. In this, Newman and Cameron are one: converts both, ruthless in their love for intellectual precision, religious without ever being pietistic.

> [Newman] wanted Catholics to come out of the ghetto and take their place in the world, to adapt themselves, to enlarge their minds in the confidence that truth could never contradict truth, and to be guided like responsible [people] by their duly enlightened consciences. His views on faith, on free discussion, on the Church as a Communion, on the place of the laity whether in the Church or in the world, and many other points....He has supreme confidence in the power of truth, yet his defense is humble, and does not pander to intellectualism at the expense of mystery. His life was a sacrifice for the truth.[2]

Were he alive now, Cameron would manifestly and aggressively demur at any such noble association with Newman. But he would be wrong.

And so my relationship with a dead Victorian cardinal began, auspiciously, with a former Marxist intellectual. I was on solid if not familiar ground. And Newman, initially mediated by Cameron, has been the lodestone of my intellectual life as a Catholic ever since.

But Newman is, as the Tennyson scholar Peter Hinchcliffe said to me, a "slippery fellow." This was not said pejoratively but descriptively. Newman's capacity to navigate the perilous shoals of Anglican political collisions, Roman curial machinations, and the shifting philosophical priorities of the day make him a model of ecclesiastical survival in our own day—my day.

Newman's life makes for endlessly fascinating and instructive reading. We see him at all the points of intersection of the various and often combative religious and intellectual currents of our very distinctly non-Victorian twenty-first century. Arguments, indeed, over whether Newman is a conservative, traditionalist, liberal, or progressive occupy the attention of the variegated Roman Catholic theological spectrum. For some, Newman is the consummate organ of orthodoxy and, for others, the subtle paragon of subversion; for some, he is the final breakwater before the waves of modernity, indeed postmodernity, inundate the church, and for others, he is the one slyly putting holes in the dykes.

No matter what labels we affix to Newman, the slippery fellow eludes them. They fail to embrace the creative complexity of his mind. The Anglican scholar and historian Owen Chadwick said it best in his introduction to Susan Foister's National Portrait Gallery of Great Britain publication, *Cardinal Newman 1801–1890: A Centenary Exhibition*:

> This conservative as he seemed at first sight to be, was an innovator struggling to change the habits and ideas of the community of

> which he was a member, and discovering like any reformer that a lot of the other members resented being invited to change their habits or ideas. Wherever he went he gathered disciples and enemies, but, like reformers generally, more of the second than the first.[3]

What were some of these ideas and habits that he struggled to change? What is at the heart of Newman's innovative genius? In addressing these questions, I want to alight on the four primary components of the Newman legacy: his championing of the laity; his thinking on the proper function of, respectively, the university/theological academy and the Magisterium; his contemplative spirituality; his spirited defense of conscience.

In the process of doing so we will discover how much the conservative innovates and how much the innovator conserves.

II

"WHO ARE THE LAITY?"

Ian Ker, the Newman biographer, provides as fine an insight into the nature of Newman's thinking as can be found anywhere:

> The mind of Newman is characterized not by contradictions but by complementary strengths, so that he may be called, without inconsistency, both conservative and liberal, progressive and traditional, cautious and radical, dogmatic yet pragmatic, idealistic but realistic.[1]

The resourcefulness, catholicity, and intricacy of this very supple mind were severely taxed by the myopia of the Roman mentality, a clerical mentality fueled by fear, secrecy, hostility to the questioning mind, unswerving adherence to an ecclesiology resistant to any change. His collisions with the church establishment were the most intense when it came to the role of the laity.

It all started with *The Rambler*, a journal that was founded by the Oxford convert J. M. Capes and jointly edited with Richard Simpson, another convert. In time, no less than the future Lord Acton, one of the titans of nineteenth-century Catholic thought, would join their ranks. Embroiled in controversy from the outset around the type and tone of the essays and reviews they published—its aim was to restore the intellectual integrity and viability of Catholicism in a non-Catholic world by showcasing work of the highest professional and scholarly standards—the editors faced episcopal wrath and lay incomprehension. Newman became engaged in the life of *The Rambler*, trying to keep at bay the censure of the bishops. Increasingly, he was drawn into the vortex of what would become *The Rambler* Affair. A flurry of delations and denunciations ensued; Newman replaced Simpson as editor, in great part in order to guarantee its continuance in an acrimonious atmosphere; and then things worsened. Theological criticism from a professor of theology at Ushaw, Dr. John Gillow; the machinations of the ever-intriguing Msgr. George Talbot, Newman's archenemy in Roman circles fanning the flames of suspicion against Newman; the timidity of Newman's bishop, William Ullathorne; and the corrosive skepticism of England's premier prelate, Nicholas Wiseman, ever wary of Newman's motives and ambitions, all combined to create an environment wherein the trust necessary for the flourishing of the journal was lethally compromised.

Simpson would eventually lash out in the context of the English Catholic bishops' adamant resistance to cooperating with a national commission on elementary education. Their resistance to the objectives and mode of operating of the commission provoked a spasm of outrage in a letter Simpson wrote, initially intended for publication in *Le Correspondant*, a review published by the French Catholic intellectual Charles Forbes René de Montalembert:

> Jealousy of the laity is a natural result of the strictness of the administrative organization which is now considered to constitute the strength of the clergy....The compactness of the clerical union makes it a caste; it has a separate professional education and separate habits of thought....The laity are to be kept in ignorance of all religious questions except those in the catechism, in order to misuse their obedience

> to a body of directors professionally educated to manage their religion for them. Religion is turned into administration, the clergy into theological police, & the body of thinking laymen into a mass of *suspects*, supposed to be brooding on nothing but revolution, & only kept together by motives of fear, & by the external pressure of a clerical organization.[2]

Simpson's tirade is more than justified, and Newman shared his deep disappointment with an ecclesiastical system that devalued the laity, but Newman moved more cautiously in his efforts to secure a future for *The Rambler*—that is, until it became necessary to directly confront hierarchical intransigence, to directly confront the disparagement of the laity that was the gruel that kept clerical entitlement sated.

Newman's bishop once asked him, "Who are the laity?" And he responded something to the effect that the church would look foolish without them. Bishop Ullathorne's query was more puzzled and benign compared to Msgr. Talbot's rather pointed and malign "What is the province of the laity? To hunt, to shoot, to entertain. These matters they understand, but to meddle with ecclesiastical matters they have no right at all."[3]

It was necessary to set the record straight. To provide an argument that would compel church leaders to attend to the charisms of the laity, to provide the laity itself with a raison d'être not dependent on the shifting sands of clerical approval, and to do all of this by means of a reclamation of the historical record, a *ressourcement* that would ground the continuing importance of the laity to the life of the church that is constitutive rather than ancillary or marginal.

On Consulting the Faithful in Matters of Doctrine, published in the same year as Charles Darwin's *On the Origin of Species by Means of Natural Selection, or the Preservation of Favoured Races in the Struggle for Life*—1859—would have in its more restricted world a similarly proportionate effect on settled thinking. Such texts as these were Copernican in their influence in their time and in our own.

Newman was never more potent in argument nor convincing in his rhetorical gifts for suasion than when under attack. He knew how to marshal his ideas, how to ground them in fact and precedent, what analogies best to employ to strengthen his position, and he knew the intellectual deficiencies in the shoddy architecture of his opponents' arguments. He was best when poised to strike. Not that he was eager for contestation for its own sake, or that he treasured the opportunity to eviscerate his detractors and enemies—and he had plenty of both—but because his mind was best when most alert, his temperament finely crafted for vigorous interaction. Truth unfolds in fierce dialogue. It is, as he once said, "wrought out by many minds, working together freely."

This is not to say that Newman was a confirmed cerebralist, existing only in his mind, his life and opinions shaped by the relentless application of syllogism and deductive reasoning. He knew that we know in diverse ways and that the mode of knowing associated with the heart, often relegated to an inferior status, succeeds when logic fails:

> The heart is commonly reached, not through the reason, but through the imagination, by means of direct impressions, by the testimony of facts and events, by history, by description. Persons influence us, voices melt us, looks subdue us, deeds inflame us....Logic makes a sorry rhetoric with the multitude; first shoot round corners, and you may not despair of converting by a syllogism....I say plainly I do not want to be converted by a smart syllogism; if I am asked to convert others by it, I say plainly I do not care to overcome their reason without touching their hearts.[4]

Very Pascalian in makeup and reasoning, Newman exalted the ways of the mind but not at the expense of the whole person. Still, when the occasion commanded a full-throttle debate, he was ever ready, ready with his data, queries, and firm probings, energized by the urgency of the moment.

And there was urgency when he wrote *On Consulting the Faithful in Matters of Doctrine*. The assaults on *The Rambler* and on him—his sensitivity antennae were on high alert—prompted him to respond by advancing the notion that the laity are indeed not a decorative element of the church, a grouping easily dismissed as inconsequential when it comes to the matter of faith and ecclesiastical governance.

The best way to demonstrate this point was to unearth historical facts buried under centuries of inattention (that's the less contentious reading) or through the deliberate suppression of uncomfortable truths (that's the more provocative reading). Either way, Newman was determined to set the record straight.

Newman draws on a careful assemblage of relevant historical incidents to show the value of that branch of evidence that derives from the "*fidelium sensus* and *consensus*...which it is natural or necessary for the Church to regard and consult, before she proceeds to any definition, from its intrinsic cogency."[5]

The laity, he proposed, held firm when episcopal authority wavered and theological opinion collapsed into the din of Babel. There is a voice for the laity, and there is a place for the laity, not only in articulating *the sense of the faith*, but in providing an intelligent and critical *reception* of church teaching:

> I think I am right in saying that the tradition of the Apostles, committed to the whole Church in its various constituents and functions *per modum unius*, manifests itself variously at various times: sometimes by the mouth of the episcopacy, sometimes by the doctors, sometimes by the people, sometimes by liturgies, rites, ceremonies, and customs, by events, disputes, movements, and all those other phenomena which are comprised under the name of history. It follows that none of these channels of tradition may be treated with disrespect; granting at the same time fully, that the gift of discerning, discriminating, defining, promulgating, and enforcing any portion of that tradition resides solely in the *Ecclesia docens* [the church teaching].[6]

It was never enough for Newman to advance an idea, a proposition, without providing concrete historical instances to buttress his position. And so, after making his theoretical case, he dipped into the chest of historical items to substantiate his case. He outlined four specific historical moments when the laity "saved" the church. The councils of the fourth century called into question the divinity of Jesus, and the laity denounced the impugners of Christ's divine nature. In a later time, when Benedictine monks from France and Germany were much exercised in their disputes around the Real Presence, the laity rallied behind Paschasius, a Carolingian abbot and theologian of the ninth century, in his defense of the teaching. It was the faithful who stood behind Pope John XXII, the fourteenth-century Avignon pontiff, in affirming the beatitude of the saints in heaven though so many questioned it. And it was a more contemporary example of its instantiation that climaxed his list of lay muscle-flexing: when Pope Pius IX was moved to formally declare as a dogma of the faith the Immaculate Conception of the Blessed Virgin Mary in 1854, in spite of having the support of the universal episcopacy, nonetheless canvassed widely to know the feelings of the laity on the doctrine prior to its promulgation.

In a later text—the appendix to the third edition of his *The Arians of the Fourth Century*—Newman reminds his readers of the visceral fidelity of the laity in sharp contrast to the disabling fractiousness of the church leaders. The history immediately following the Council of Nicaea in the fourth century and the residual aftershocks of the stubborn heresy of Arianism combined to show a weak church leadership in contrast with a resilient but tenaciously orthodox laity. The governed, Newman asserted, were the true champions of Catholic truth while the bishops failed to distinguish themselves. It was the laity who were, in Newman's view, the preeminent ones, zealous, not without courage in confronting the assailants of orthodoxy, and steadfast.

From Newman's perspective, the historical case is fully defensible. And if the church governors fail to heed the yearning of the laity—a yearning articulated poignantly in the writings of educated laity—the consequences are extreme. He makes that point with special emphasis in the concluding paragraph of *On Consulting the Faithful in Matters of Doctrine*:

> I think certainly that the *Ecclesia docens* is more happy when she has such enthusiastic partisans about her...than when she cuts off the faithful from the study of her divine doctrines and the sympathy of her divine contemplations, and requires from them a *fides implicita* in her word, which in the educated classes will terminate in indifference, and in the poorer in superstition.[7]

Newman's manifesto on the full incorporation of the laity in the thinking of the church was not received well in the circles of power. It is still not. Yet the study of theology, canon law, church history, and spirituality (traditionally taught in seminaries as ascetical theology for centuries) are no longer the exclusive preserve of the ordained; indeed, in many jurisdictions enrollment in the "sacred sciences" has tipped in favor of laywomen and retreat directors in various of the Catholic spiritual traditions as numbers of fully credentialled laypersons have mushroomed with consistently impressive success. It is no longer uncommon to find canonical positions such as diocesan chancellors filled by able laypeople.

Undoubtedly, the Catholic laity, post–Second Vatican Council, is seen in even the highest ecclesiastical sectors as much more than agents, to use Talbot's dismissive summary, of hunting, praying, and obeying. I have never cared to hunt, praying is an inexhaustibly difficult task, and obeying does not come naturally to me, so I fail dismally under all three rubrics.

III

NEWMAN, MODEL FOR CONTEMPORARY CATHOLIC INTELLECTUALS

Fortunately, schooled in Newman via Cameron, I have come to appreciate the genuine range of lay contribution to church life and especially to recognize that the danger of having one's faith terminate in indifference is omnipresent. We must be vigilant. Discouragement with hierarchical intransigence over the ongoing clerical sex abuse scandals, frustration with the residual hold of clericalism among those who abjure the "evil of clericalism" but continue to live in its nurturing womb, catatonic resistance to full inclusion of women into the ordained ministries, antipathy toward a papacy that privileges mercy over dogma, and the stubborn resurgence of movements among the laity designed to shore up the *ancien régime* because of devotional conservatism, reactionary politics, or theological obscurantism are just some of the pathologies that infect the church.

Closing our mind to the imperative of radical reform is a false comfort. So is the temptation to reduce Catholicism to its dysfunctionality. Newman loved the church, despite its array of wounds, its defensiveness, and its fears. He knew that truth emerges out of the collision of intellects, that communion defeats sectarianism, that the imagination can be a vehicle of grace, that spiritual companionship is more than succor: it is life-generating for the mind and for the heart.

Critical to so much of the right-thriving of Catholicism is the high value Newman attached to education. To that end, Newman has been my guide as a student, college teacher, university professor, faculty dean, vice president, and president and vice chancellor of two universities. He has shaped my thinking on liberal arts, the pastoral function of the university, the role of the humanities in higher education, the relationship of the church to university, the mission of a Catholic university in reference to the cultivation of a vibrant Catholic public intellectual life, and the importance of learning to the enrichment and ennobling of social and political life.

Newman remains my antidote, my intellectual serum, to the poison that courses through many higher education circles, the uncritical acceptance of the Shavian dogma that a Catholic university is a contradiction in terms, an oxymoron, because a free mind cannot coexist with Roman certitude. This is a caricature, of course, but like all caricatures, there is a profound kernel of truth at its core.

How do we disabuse our scholarly colleagues who subscribe to George Bernard Shaw's impish quip? How do we show that a vital intellectual questing is not inconsistent with a self-critical religious faith? And how do we live out—personally, professionally, and institutionally—a creed that expands the intellectual and spiritual horizons of our students without easy rationalizing, skillful avoidance, or unthreatening simplification?

Newman faced all the above challenges, and in the manner of his response to these challenges, we can find a way for Catholic higher education in our own time, not by simulating the idyllic enclosure of a mid-nineteenth-century Oxbridge college, or by recapturing the male elitism of a Victorian public school education, or by promoting a Catholic higher education revival tied to a romantic mixing of establishment privilege with Catholic orthodoxy.

Newman's life is testament to a very different trajectory.

Newman wrote extensively about education—*Discourses on the Scope and Nature of University Education Addressed to the Catholics of Dublin* (1852); *Offices and Works of Universities* (1856); *Lectures and Essays on University Subjects* (1859).

For Newman the church founds a university, not to celebrate genius, the wide acquisition of knowledge, or the cultivation of talent, but because of pastoral solicitude and the need to provide a spiritual underpinning for the lives of the students, to shape them for leadership in society, to create a space for their right flourishing.

In his work for the Catholics of Dublin—given that he had been invited to create a university in a corner of the English realm that was traditionally hostile to educating Catholics—Newman was clear on distinguishing between academies and universities and between the quite discrete functions of discovering and of teaching. He was aware that the Holy See's efforts to establish through the Irish hierarchy a Catholic university for English-speaking Catholics was a form of historical redress. The advantages enjoyed by Protestants should be available to Catholics as well.

This was the time—the 1850s—when he was directly

involved in establishing a university in Dublin, an undertaking that proved to be much more fraught and complicated than he could have expected. It was to serve as his rough entrée into the world of ecclesiastical politics, jealously guarded hierarchical prerogatives, jurisdictional squabbles, and a pervasive and ingrained clerical anti-intellectualism.

His years as founder and first rector were riddled with intrigue, misperception, distrust, and pettiness. He was initially approached by Paul Cullen, archbishop of Armagh and eventually cardinal archbishop of Dublin, to undertake the onerous task of establishing the university. It was a project designed to offset the damage anticipated by the Queen's University of Ireland initiative of Sir Robert Peel with its secular, nondenominational, and mixed education components.

From the outset, Newman was persuaded of the primary involvement of the laity; he was resolved that although he would be appointed rector, the management of the university would be shared with a predominantly lay faculty. In part, this structure was conceived as being essentially different from St. Patrick's College, the national seminary of Maynooth, and would remind all who need reminding that a university is not a clerical redoubt.

Newman's troubles with Cullen were legendary, and the protracted negotiations drained the English convert of much of his valuable energy. Still resident most of the year at his Birmingham Oratory, Newman was compelled to travel constantly to satisfy his several commitments, and the tardiness and anxiety of the Irish hierarchy greatly compounded the already considerable labors of founding and directing a university. To the Irish episcopacy he was a dubious entity at best. After all, he was not a cradle Catholic, and he was English to boot.

In his *Autobiographical Writings* Newman disclosed his realization that at the heart of the friction that existed between Cullen and himself was his determination to make the laity the "substantive power in the university." After all, Newman was convinced that the financial governance of the university must be vested in the hands of those for whom it was intended. He was, however, acutely aware that such a notion ran counter to the less-than-venerable Irish clerical convention that would have the laity infantilized.

Newman's intention to appoint honorary members of the university drawn from the laity—in addition to appointing competent laypersons to all the professorial chairs, save theology—could not but provoke an obscurantist hierarchy.

At the opening of the new university church, Newman preached a sermon titled "Intellect, the Instrument of Religious Training," outlining his purpose as rector:

> It will not satisfy me, what satisfies so many, to have two independent systems, intellectual and religious, going at once side by side, by a sort of division of labour, and only accidently brought together. It will not satisfy me, if religion is here, and science there, and young men converse with science all day, and lodge with religion in the evening....I want the same roof to contain both the intellectual and moral discipline. Devotion is not a sort of finish given to the sciences; nor is science a sort of feather in the cap, if I may so express myself, an ornament and set—off to devotion. *I want the intellectual layman to be religious, and the devout ecclesiastic to be intellectual.*[1]

Persuaded of the need to contain the clerical presence at the university rather than expand it, Newman found himself at odds with the general thinking of his ecclesiastical superiors. It is *not* that Newman had an exaggerated respect for the lay state or a penchant for cleric-bashing; he simply held to a historical perspective that refused to suppress the charism or essential uniqueness of the lay vocation in the interests of a clericalized ecclesiology.

The university qua university—whether in Dublin or elsewhere—is for the enlargement of the sensibility, the cultivation of the mind, and the uncompromised pursuit of intellectual excellence. But these are not bodiless exploits, somehow untouched by the personal, the pastoral, and the moral. Newman understood the irreplaceable value of human interaction, for, as he argues in *Historical Sketches*, volume 1, "an academical system without the personal influence of teachers upon pupils, is an arctic winter; it will create an ice-bound, petrified, cast-iron university."[2]

The university has as its function intellectual culture:

> to open the mind, to correct it, to refine it, to enable it to know, and to digest, master, rule, and use its knowledge to give it power over its own faculties, application, flexibility, method, critical exactness, sagacity, resource, address, eloquent expression.[3]

The utter bankruptcy of an education that does not touch the moral fiber of a person has been dramatically etched in the terrifying apotheosis of twentieth-century barbarism: the Wagner-loving, Goethe-reading culture of the supreme automaton—the concentration camp commander. George Steiner, Hannah Arendt, Thomas Merton, and Eli Mandel have analyzed with positively unnerving honesty the severe limitations of reason. When the educated person is devoid of a humane sensibility, an active conscience, an ennobling intelligence, then the horrors visited upon us by the purveyors of unchecked power are even greater and offer no salvation.

We have known this dark landscape and know that it is not confined to the conflagrations of the two great wars. Genocide, unaccountable autocratic power, savage reprisals, political chicanery, the drastic drought of truth that is universal in its reach, and the ascendency of a renegade power of celebrity all contribute to a coarsening of society and usurpation of virtue in the political orbit.

For Newman, the rank utilitarianism of nineteenth-century political culture—full-blown in our own time—could in great measure be countered by university culture wherein the intellect is cultivated not denigrated, wherein it is disciplined and not held hostage to the exigencies of the moment and the demands of economic pragmatism. It is a sanctuary, an oasis, a sacred grove where curiosity and intellectual disinterestedness function as an antidote to the madding crowd of realists, pragmatists, and university functionaries that see the learning place as a recruitment center.

Henri Nouwen, the Dutch priest and psychologist who spent many years teaching variously at the University of Notre Dame, Yale, Harvard, Boston College, and Regis College in the Toronto School of Theology, has written in an impassioned way—everything Nouwen did was impassioned—about his souring on the quality, timbre, motivations, and élan of higher education.

In *Lifesigns: Intimacy, Fecundity, and Ecstasy in Christian Perspective*, Nouwen lamented the sad compulsiveness of his students: pressured, indifferent to the pleasures induced by contemplation, driven by a relentless competition for the highest honors, obsessed with "deliverables, quantifiables, and measurables," and incapable of satiety. They are productive without being fertile; they commodify their learning in the interests of their employability; the university is not a place of joy, rest, and unhurried meditation. It is, rather, a revved-up engine propelled by the sheer force of its desperate relevance. For Nouwen—and Newman was one of his most important spiritual and intellectual mentors—universities have drifted far from their *raison d'être*:

> The word "school," which comes from *schola* (meaning: free time), reminds us that schools were originally meant to interrupt a busy existence and create some space to contemplate the mysteries of life. Today they have become the arena for a hectic race to accomplish as much as possible, and to acquire in a short period the necessary tools to survive the great battle of human life. Books written to be savored slowly are read hastily to fulfill a requirement, painting

> made to be seen with a contemplative eye are taken in as part of a necessary art appreciation course, and music composed to be enjoyed at leisure is listened to in order to identify a period or style. Thus, colleges and universities meant to be places for quiet learning have become places of fierce competition, in which the rewards go to those who produce the most and best.[4]

For Newman, the productivity versus fecundity antithesis deployed by Nouwen is most starkly articulated in his *Discourses on the Scope and Nature of University Education Addressed to the Catholics of Dublin* when he confronts those advocates of economic pragmatism who

> insist that education should be confined to some particular and narrow end, and should issue in some definite work, which can be weighed and measured....This they call making education and instruction "useful," and "utility" becomes their watchword. With a fundamental principle of this nature, they very naturally go on to ask what there is to show for the expense of a university; what is the real worth in the market of the article called liberal education, on the supposition that it does not teach us

> definitely how to advance our manufacturers, or to improve our lands, or to better our civil economy; or again, if it does at once make this man a lawyer, that an engineer, and that a surgeon; or at least if it does not lead to discoveries in chemistry, astronomy, geology, magnetism, and science of every kind.[5]

Who has not heard this before? As a professor, department chair, associate dean, dean, vice president, and president, to say nothing of being a father with four children who were bound for tertiary-level education, I have felt the trepidation of those embarked on an education track outside of a professional orbit, unsure of what they intend to be, nervous that courses that interest them will be a mere indulgence and apprehensive that an education without utility is a career death trap. Consequently, I have found myself struggling to provide an intellectually credible antidote to the poison of careerism, the watertight arguments of the pragmatists, the firm ground of the utilitarians.

Newman's answer became my own: the university is not a storage hold from which can be drawn a fully equipped work force. It is, rather, "according to the usual designation, an Alma Mater, knowing her children one by one, not a foundry, or a mint, or a treadmill."[6]

It is still a hard sell; financial considerations are not

peripheral and often paramount; parental investments and expectations cannot be lightly relegated to an ancillary role in shaping the future of their children; social pressures and market viability in a gig economy are major factors determining academic choices.

But the essentials of Newman's teaching on education—higher education, specifically—remain relevant. His pastoral approach, however, is certainly not in vogue on most campuses; the tutor-student relationship as defined by his Oxbridge experience is far removed from the average North American undergraduate pedagogical experience; theology is perceived in most secular institutions as suspect and in many Catholic institutions as problematic; and the very notion of intellectual disinterestedness is the stuff of nostalgia, fantasy, or subversive ideation. Yet, Newman is quoted regularly and approvingly by university bureaucrats incapable of establishing his ideas as normative, ecclesiastics invoke his authority selectively, and most value him as the newly raised to the altars holy one worthy of devotion but an eccentric withal.

But what of those essentials then?

Newman provides the blueprint for a critical, wondrously curious, undiluted pursuit of truth, no matter how provisional, and in doing so creates a firewall against the allurements of spin doctors, "reputation advocates," lobbyists, propagandists, and newsmakers without conscience and integrity. Newman would have us cultivate the intellect in such a way as to allow us to submit to unmuddled scrutiny the ideological biases, spurious presuppositions, and quasi-authentic analyses that proffer an easy wisdom in an age hellbent on the instant remedy for headache and ennui.

In this regard, J. M. Cameron excoriates the educated citizenry for its mad credulousness, its generally unreflective approach to ideas and modes of thinking, its capacity to be duped. At various times, whether in his published essays, book reviews, and especially in public lectures and in class, Cameron would mock the frightening credulousness of a group he termed the "lumpen intellectuals." That is, students and faculty who have embraced the maddeningly irrational beliefs of the day: astrology, speaking to flowers (although he would likely rethink his categorical denunciation of this current lunacy in light of the astonishing work done on the subject of tree communication by ecologist Suzanne Simard), and most dangerous, less ludicrous, the specious scientific evidence advanced for different racial theories. Cameron could easily add to the list: the resurgence of a fascist mentality that thrives on group conformity, whether with campus censuring mechanisms or political populism, the proliferation of anti-God polemics dressed up with a patina of scientific respectability (Dawkins, et al.), and theological revisionism that holds

Catholic thinkers like Gilbert Keith Chesterton hostage, diluting the quality of their work in the interests of an urgent polemic to protect the church from those who would sunder it from within.

When George Steiner in *Nostalgia for the Absolute* speaks of surrogate or substitute theologies filling the vacuum left by the evacuation of reigning orthodoxies or normative belief systems in society, the rise of quasi-legitimate sciences—creationism, for instance, or conversion therapy—as well as the proliferation of political creeds that mock facticity and celebrate self-serving fiction as the new modality, we are not far from Cameron's critique.

It is the job, as Newman argues, of education to produce fair critics of both received and untried ideas. And that includes for Catholic universities sound critiques of religion—its myriad institutional roles, its checkered and complex history, its capacity to either expand or diminish human freedom—precisely because the academy, particularly an academy grounded in a faith tradition, is called to be a guarantor, perhaps *the* guarantor, of intellectual freedom.

In a time when political chambers and the halls of commerce profess only a minimalist commitment to the ideals of a higher education liberated from a utilitarian objective, recovering Newman isn't just an exercise in historical memory. Recovering Newman is a way of salvaging from the ruins a more humane though tough approach to our curriculum, our various teaching styles, and our educational vision. We do this by assessing all claims to truth under the rigorous lens of an exacting scrutiny; we underscore the centrality of independent as opposed to group thinking; we eschew the clichés and opaque jargon that frame a patina of wisdom; and we cultivate a hermeneutic of suspicion.

IV

NEWMAN TODAY

If Newman is a model for the contemporary Catholic public intellectual, and I am firmly convinced that he is, he needs to be evaluated in a way that doesn't limit him to his own century, that doesn't confine him to the corridors of sanctity where he is inaccessible to all but the devout, and that doesn't lionize him as a reverent figure—even for the nonbelievers—an endlessly interesting churchman with political and religious survival skills.

Newman deserves better.

Given the dearth of credible public Catholic intellectuals in our time—at least in the Anglosphere and more pointedly in the United States and Canada—Newman's appeal is all the greater. There are reasons for the decline—at least in profile—of avowedly Catholic public intellectuals: decades of caution have produced timorous scholars; temerity is punished and conformity rewarded; two pontificates that shaped Catholic academic life for decades have produced a parched intellectual landscape; secular hostility to Catholic thought has increased in proportion to the perception, and indeed reality, of suppression and censure meted out by ecclesiastical authorities; sharp and probing minds elect to study and acquire expertise in areas less likely to be turbulent and threatening to their careers in academe; the reduced presence in the non-Catholic media of Catholics willing to claim the identifier "Catholic"; the loss of confidence in articulating a Catholic perspective in a period of incendiary claims of disloyalty by the self-appointed monitors of truth; an episcopate that is anti-intellectual at worst and composed mostly of apparatchiks keen on the party line, especially the old party line; the foreclosing of the Catholic mind.

The renascence of Catholic intellectual life that existed *êntre-deux-guerres* in the United Kingdom and on the continent and the flowering of Catholic thought and letters in parts of Canada and the United States after the Second World War have not been replicated in recent decades.

The foreclosing of the Catholic mind—contraction, defensiveness, timidity—during the Wojtyla and Ratzinger pontificates, even more ironic given the intellectual fecundity of both, would not have been unknown to Newman. The papacy of Pius IX—although not without its achievements—was reactionary in the extreme. If Benedict XVI had his 1968, Pio Nono had his 1848, and in both cases Catholic intellectuals would pay a heavy price.

After all, it was Newman who opined that popes can live too long, their prolonged tenure a danger to the health of the church. What is essential is the free interchange of ideas—an interchange by means of which truth emerges. This interchange is not an exercise in one-upmanship, culminating in the overthrow of an opponent's argument; it is not an exercise in ecclesial partisanship, dividing Christ by transmuting one's private opinions into declared doctrine. It is, rather, "a collision of intellects," struggling to produce a deeper understanding of what is known, of what is believed—an evolving and historical approach in keeping with philosopher and theologian Bernard Lonergan's understanding of the dramatic shift in human consciousness from the classicist to the historicist. Lonergan would write, many decades after the death of Newman, but always inspired by his epistemological insights in Newman's late work *A Grammar of Assent*, and in that sense extending Newman's critique of the inadequacies of shoring up a desiccated truth:

> Classical culture has given way to modern culture, and, I would submit, the crisis of our age

> is in no small measure the fact that modern culture has not yet reached its maturity. The classical mediation of meaning has broken down, the breakdown has been effected by a whole array of new and more effective techniques; but their very multiplicity and complexity leave us bewildered, disorientated, confused, preyed-upon by anxiety, dreading lest we fall victims to the up-to-date myth of ideology, and the hypnotic, highly effective magic of thought control.[1]

Lonergan, an avowed disciple of Newman's, addresses the shift from a classicist to historicist mentality differently but in continuity. Newman's recognition in his numerous writings that a static understanding of the dogmatic principle diminishes our ability to apprehend truth, his insistence on a return to the sources, and his openness to contemporary thinking—unlike most of his contemporaries Newman found Darwin more an invitation to new thinking than a threat to the heart of religion, as evidenced by his letter to Canon J. Walker in May 1868:

> If Mr. Darwin in this or that point of his theory comes into collision with revealed truth, that is another matter—but I do not see that the *principle* of development, or what I have called

> construction, does....Mr. Darwin's theory *need* not then be atheistical, be it true or not; it may simply be suggesting a larger idea of Divine Prescience and Skill.[2]

Newman's keen attention to the secular—his refusal to engage in either deriding or dismissing the new or novel—situates him as an ideal exemplar for the Catholic intellectual. Rather than moving into defensive mode—the standard approach in the Roman School and the seminary system to every perceived threat to the established way of doing things, the established way of believing things—Newman's approach was to attend, to listen, to probe, and then to fiercely defend when necessary. He would have no truck with every passing notion; he was neither faddish nor latitudinarian in temperament or intellectual disposition. But he wasn't frightened of fresh thinking. After all, his preferred modus operandi was the collision of intellects, and they need not be only Catholic intellect in collision with Catholic intellect. Yes, he could be an apologist of the most persuasive kind. After all, the *Apologia pro Vita Sua* is his studied, eloquent, and brilliant response to the calumny hurled at him by popular novelist and churchman Charles Kingsley that the Roman clergy have a well-demonstrated taste for equivocation. And yes, he could be set afire by theological controversies that he thought imperiled the well-being of the church and the commonweal, but his reasoned approach to suasion was colored by his spirituality, a spirituality that was quasi-monastic.

Newman, as mediated by Cameron, provides for me a model for the contemporary Catholic educator trying to make sense of the considerable array of challenges in the digital age because he never abandons the pastoral dimension of educating the young, never diminishes the role of theology in the curriculum of the university, and never acts arbitrarily when dealing with his charges, his faculty, and his superiors. Without invoking the terms—in both cases, anachronistically, given their definition and subsequent development—Newman incorporated the principles of collegiality and subsidiarity in his educational thinking and leadership.

These two key concepts together provide a critical antidote to creeping managerialism and can, by means of an imaginative reappropriation, provide the foundation stones for genuine coresponsibility in academic governance. This is what, I believe, Newman tried to realize with his Dublin university project, only to encounter resistance at almost every level. But a contemporary adaptation of his thinking could go a long way in inspiring the higher educational establishment to explore new ways of *being* a university for the twenty-first century.

Combined, collegiality and subsidiarity can guarantee—to the degree that such is possible and only ever provisionally—that the university engage in the larger social enterprise of creating not just a knowledge and data accumulation culture but a wisdom culture. One of the persistent challenges facing higher education is the diversification of its delivery models—frightful parasense, I know—and although we can rise above the argot, *delivery* is the right term in the end. It seems to me that the digital-age university has the unique opportunity of recapturing the particular genius of the medieval university and the Oxbridge model, thereby incorporating aspects of an earlier teaching modality and of rethinking the function of knowledge creation itself in ways that are supportive of a more deeply enriched human enterprise.

> Knowledge transmission via the internet provides a wonderful opportunity to re-conceive the role of the tutor/mentor as opposed to the narrowly conceived definition of the magister still dominant in our institutions of higher education. The teacher [as Newman knew and modeled] is more than an instructor; the teacher in the digital age is a guide and mentor. The challenges facing Western universities in particular in terms of a reconfiguration of post-secondary education goals can, if only left to the mandarins of industry and government, result in a further commodification of learning and not in

> the making of a wisdom culture. To help effect the creation of this culture, presidents and principals of Catholic institutions of higher education should themselves be seen as public intellectuals, and universities as sanctuaries. The only way we can provide a meaningfully credible definition of the university in the twenty-first century is to dig deeply into our past, unearth concepts and practices that can be revitalized and recontextualized, respond to the learning of the ancients [and the Schoolmen] in ways that speak to the timeless dimension of knowledge.[3]

Newman's educational philosophy is not an exercise in Victorian thought alone; it is not an arcane body of reflection predicated on his privileged tertiary-level education in nineteenth-century England; and it is not circumscribed by his limited exposure to academic administration. All these play their part, of course, but Newman's insights around the ingredients that make for an ideal paradigm transcend chronology. His thinking would be in sync with that of Thomas Aquinas whose assertion that the

> beatitude—blessed are those who mourn—is the special beatitude for those whose calling

> it is to extend the boundaries of knowledge—for intellectuals, in other words. St. Thomas's assertion is to say the least of it, intriguing, and naturally provokes one to ask why intellectuals are to be classed as those who mourn. The answer Thomas gives is that, whenever our minds yearn towards some new truth, then we become afflicted with pain, because our whole being wishes to protect the inertia and comfort which we have established for ourselves; and the pain is the symptom of our distress at its disturbance. Moreover, we experience a sort of bereavement when those formulations, images and symbols have, over the years, become part of ourselves. And we mourn that loss as we would mourn the loss of a limb.[4]

The intellectual life as a life of mourning? Only in so far as it reminds us of its tentativeness, its provisionality, its false solace, its complacency and comfort with the known, the established, the familiar tools of the trade. But every new truth, every adjustment to our knowing, engenders hope at the same time as it engenders grieving. Intellectuals are the sentinels and only humility inoculates against hubris.

Newman would be in agreement with Aquinas on the beatitude that applies most fittingly to those engaged in the intellectual life, for after all his learning was grounded in a life of interiority as much as it was lived out in the public forum. Newman's life was a life of spiritual attention, contemplative practice, and rigorous discipline.

V

NEWMAN, MERTON, AND THE RETURN TO THE SOURCES

If my understanding of Newman's formidable intellectual contributions was built on my studies with Cameron, my appreciation of Newman's spirituality was built on my doctoral work on the monk-poet Thomas Merton.

My dissertation on Merton, eventually published as *Heretic Blood: The Spiritual Geography of Thomas Merton*, was an examination of Merton's literary corpus—consisting of ten volumes of verse, a radio play, a novel, and numerous essays—as interpreted through the lens of William Blake, poet, visionary, visual artist, and exotic savant. Blake was the presiding genius of Merton's life, the subject of his master's thesis at Columbia University, a constant in his diaries and essays, an enduring link with his artist-father, Owen, a figure who opened Merton to the *visionary* mode of knowing, in keeping with similar poets like Henry Vaughan, Thomas Traherne, Christopher Smart, and W. B. Yeats.

In many ways Merton, a genuinely extraterritorial writer, wrote and thought outside restrictive boundaries. Born in France and educated there and in England prior to moving to the birthplace of his mother, the United States, in the 1930s, Merton had a deeply Gallican but also even more deeply English sensibility. Newman was a natural. And reading Merton *on* Newman deepened my understanding of both.

I recall the peculiar circumstances when I alighted on this Merton-Newman connection for the first time. I was in my first year of doctoral studies and during the reading week of the university I took off for the Abbey of Gethsemani, Merton's monastic home for nearly three decades, to spend the time checking out the sources. In 1973, many of Merton's books, manuscripts, and the like, had yet to be fully moved and catalogued at Bellarmine College, now University, where they are permanently housed in the Thomas Merton Center, and I was quite thrilled with it all. The simple pleasure that comes from being virtuous—I was actually working during reading week and not lounging on some sun-drenched beach—and the even greater delight, not connected in any way with virtue, spurious or otherwise, in browsing through primary sources.

I was not accustomed to the regimen of a Trappist diet—less severe now than in 1973, and by 1973 already modified by comparison to the time of Merton's entry of 1941—so I often found myself famished, even after eating the modest fare pretending to be lunch. The monks must have known something of the weakness of most mortals staying with them on retreat—or in my case, research time—because they offered some compensation in the form of fruitcake by midafternoon.

I took very generous portions of the fruitcake, and then decided to explore the spacious grounds of the abbey. While doing so I came across a goose protecting her goslings, and she chased me off the main road. I wandered in the heavy mud (it was February), climbed over a fence to the supreme puzzlement of the observing livestock, and then, mud-bespeckled, humiliated, feeling unwell, and unnerved by that fuming goose, I made my way back to the abbey. Once there, disconsolate and bedraggled, Brother Patrick Hart, the legendary Merton secretary, commented on my sorry appearance and asked what happened. I told him. Perceptive as ever, he inquired about the fruitcake and the volume I devoured. I told him that my appetite was voracious, and I ate heartily and well. He remarked, "Well, you are feeling unwell because the fruitcake is laced with bourbon and the fence you climbed over is an electric fence." I was both inebriated and zapped. I took to my room chastened, but before I did, I glanced at the library, saw a copy of *The Seven Storey Mountain*, Merton's monumentally successful autobiography, and noticed on the flyleaf that it was favorably compared to St. Augustine's *Confessions*. And not insignificantly, the copy was adjacent to Newman's *Apologia pro Vita Sua*. Given the alphabetical gap—A for Augustine and N for Newman—I wondered if this was a sign. But then I was still suffering the aftershocks of the bourbon and the fence. But that night I thought a lot about Newman. At some point, once I finished my work on Blake and Merton, I would turn to Newman to investigate and see if there was in fact an intellectual and spiritual connection.

Merton and Newman had a lot in common. A glib comparison would disclose the following shared qualities and experiences: an English education; an Anglican ecclesial genesis; considerable literary talent; a deep intellectual restlessness; religious genius.

Both men were ardent correspondents and judicious diarists, and both understood the heavy costs of conversion to the Church of Rome. Both enjoyed public approbation, and both suffered public censure. They were celebrities, though they didn't much like it and felt the sting of success. And, significantly, both could readily acknowledge the truth of Père Humbert Clérissac, the French Dominican, who observed once to his close friend Jacques Maritain (also a very close friend of Merton's) that, although it is difficult to suffer persecution for the church, it is more difficult still to suffer persecution at the hands of the church. For Newman, it was the persistent Roman suspicion of his orthodoxy (as mentioned earlier, fed by English Ultramontanes both clerical and lay), and for Merton, it was the official publication ban imposed on all his peace writings and the growing alarm in conservative quarters over his interfaith forays.

Merton was, at first, daunted by Newman's elegance, refinement, and prodigious accomplishments. He wrote in his diary *The Sign of Jonas* that he has

> absolutely nothing in common with Cardinal Newman except for the fact that we are both converts and both wrote autobiographies. He writes beautiful prose, I write slang....But above all, I feel utterly remote from Newman's society. One look into his life makes me feel like a savage. He is completely foreign to me: speech, attitude, everything. I have none of his

> refinement. In fact, I have always scrupulously avoided refinement.[1]

This latter comment speaks to Merton's having once spurned the lushness of Cambridge University for the sootiness of Columbia University, free from the constraints of an artificial and well-polished environment for a gritty American one. Merton's romanticizing of Cambridge, and his subsequent embrace of the antithesis of a centuries-old quasi-cloistered existence with the free openness of an American urban university, proved to be the kind of neat polarity that appealed to his younger imagination. In truth, Merton was not quite the success at Clare College he anticipated, earned a serious reprimand from his godfather—the physician Tom Bennett (the same who signed the death certificate for the philosopher-mystic Simone Weil)—and was essentially exiled from Albion to less comely and judgmental shores. It had little to do with refinement or its lack and a great deal to do with immaturity. There is a reverse snobbery in all of this, an arrogance that despises breeding and perceived affectation and that confuses banality with perfection.

If the young Merton found Newman remote—supreme stylist, measured and perfect—and a reminder of the world he was required to leave, he was also aware of his own deficiencies of style, a point brought home to him with magisterial definitiveness by novelist Evelyn Waugh.

Newman was not to his taste—yet.

By the time he published his diary *Conjectures of a Guilty Bystander*, a decade after his *Jonas* entry, Merton's view of Newman had changed. He wrote of Newman, twinning him with the eminent seventeenth-century theologian, archbishop, poet, and essayist, François Fénelon, of how these two great men now

> impress themselves more and more upon my heart. I revere them deeply, though formerly I ignored and misunderstood them. What moves me is their greatness, the polish of "finished" men, masterpieces, who because they are perfect beyond the ordinary seem to have reached a stasis, a condition that is not of time. They are not of their time, or ahead of it, or behind it. They are outside of it. Indeed, they reach this condition by suffering a kind of rejection which liberates them into a realm of a final perfection, a uniqueness, a humility, a wisdom, a silence that is definitive and contains all that they have ever said. So that, even when they quietly continue to speak and write, perhaps for a few people only or for no one at all, they are saying things for everyone of all time who

> can grow to understand this peculiar type of greatness. They seem "old," and belong to the past, yet they survive indefinitely. Newman is always young.[2]

In many ways, Merton too is "always young," "saying things for everyone," and liberated in the end "into a realm of a final perfection, a uniqueness, a humility, a wisdom, a silence that is definitive and contains all that [he] has ever said."

Of all the English Roman Catholic thinkers and writers who appealed to Merton—and many of the convert generation, G. K. Chesterton, Hilaire Belloc, and Robert Hugh Benson, for instance, manifestly did not appeal to him—Newman was the one he could identify with, for there was none who was more successful in casting off the shackles of decadent Scholasticism.

Newman was enamored of the early church, a sharp student of the fathers and the diverse heresies that imperiled orthodoxy, an ecclesiologist (though he would never make such a claim) who preferred the primitive sources to the manuals of the Schoolmen. Similarly, Merton's own creative and critical efforts to recover the sources of Western monasticism—the desert fathers, Eastern monasticism, the first- and second-generation Cistercians, the seventeenth-century reform that produced the Trappists—were by way of assisting the reform and renewal of his own order in his own time. To that end, Merton, like Newman, was a "radical" theologian in the sense that he went to the roots, and like Newman, he had a particular fondness for Clement of Alexandria, whom he judged "a pioneer in Christian education, Christian humanism and even Christian mysticism."[3]

Newman's efforts to ground Anglican identity in the apostolic church—to root the tradition, as it were—were similar in kind to Merton's latter-day efforts to reacquaint the modern monk with the larger ancestry. And like Newman he refused to trifle with history. The apriorism of the Scholastics appealed to neither of them, though Merton's close association with the neo-Thomism of Jacques Maritain and Étienne Gilson—the former's *Art and Scholasticism* and the latter's *The Spirit of Medieval Philosophy* were seminal books in shaping his life and thought—helped to nuance his approach to the tradition of Aquinas, distinguishing between the vital Thomism that emerged in Europe at the beginning of the twentieth century from the atrophying manualism characteristic of the decadent Scholasticism that remained unchallenged in several Catholic quarters, though mostly resident in the seminary.

Both Newman and Merton turned to the fathers, electing monastic and historical theology over systematic. With their historical perspective they were able to distinguish the peripheral from the essential in both church doctrine and ecclesial self-understanding.

Cameron had required a close reading of Newman's *Letter to Pusey on Occasion of His Eirenicon*, and in that I discovered the special connection the early church fathers had to Newman's Catholicism:

> I am not ashamed still to take my stand upon the Fathers, and do not mean to budge. The history of their times is not yet an almanac to me....The Fathers made me a Catholic, and I am not going to kick down the ladder by which I ascended into the Church. It is a ladder quite as serviceable for that purpose now, as it was twenty years ago.[4]

Merton, too, depended on the fathers—those largely of the monastic variety—to orient his own life and spirituality. Both Newman and Merton were drawn to the fertile and creative world of the Middle Ages, rejecting a golden era or pre-Raphaelite view of the time. They loved the cut and thrust of debate, the openness to ideas—provocative and scholarly new ideas—that they saw missing in their own time. Newman put it bluntly when he wrote,

> Why was it that the Medieval Schools were so vigorous? Because they were allowed free

> and fair play—because the disputants were not made to feel the bit in their mouths at every other word they spoke, but could move their limbs freely and expatiate at will....When they went wrong, a stronger and truer intellect set them down—and, as time went on, if the dispute got perilous, and a controversialist obstinate, then at length Rome interfered—at length, *not at first—Truth is wrought out by many minds, working together freely*.[5]

Newman argued for the vital and free interplay of intellect and authority, of freedom and discipline in a way that assured the necessity of both—poised in tension—but ever struggling to apprehend the deepest truth. In a famous passage in the *Apologia pro Vita Sua*, one that Cameron had me pore over, dissecting every nuance and subtlety, Newman provides the Roman Catholic of the postconciliar era with a model of such exquisite balance and utter reasonableness that one cannot but be pained by our contemporary atmosphere of toxic mistrust:

> It is necessary for the very life of religion...that the warfare [between the claims of reason and the teaching authority of the church] should be incessantly carried on. Every exercise of Infallibility is brought out into act by an intense and

> varied operation of the Reason, both as its ally and as its opponent, and provokes again, when it has done its work, a re-action of Reason against it; and, as in civil polity the State exists and endures by means of the rivalry and collision, the encroachments and defeats of its constituent parts, so in like manner Catholic Christendom is no small exhibition of religious absolutism, but presents a continuous picture of Authority and Private Judgment alternately advancing and retreating as the ebb and flow of the tide—it is a vast assemblage of human beings with wilful intellects and wild passions, brought together into one by the beauty and the Majesty of a Superhuman Power,—into what may be called a large reformatory or training-school, not as if into a hospital or prison, not in order to be sent to bed, not to be buried alive, but (if I may change metaphor) brought together as if into some moral factory, for the melting, refining, and moulding, by an incessant noisy process, of the raw material, so excellent, so dangerous, so capable of divine purposes.[6]

Admittedly, the church as a "large reformatory" is some distance from the image of the church as "the mystical body of Christ" (Pope Pius XII) or as a "field hospital"

(Pope Francis), but it is strikingly apposite when you consider the "vast assemblage" gathered for "melting, refining and moulding." Newman knew that the finished and polished product is a phantasm—for unfinished and partial best describes our tentative grasp of the ineffable and reminds us that adoration offsets the oracular and declamatory tendencies of the academy and the perfidy of unchecked private opinion.

VI

THE CONTINUING RELEVANCE OF NEWMAN

Given the uncontained proliferation of opinion—informed or otherwise, substantive or glib—so easily facilitated by social media, the ever-ascending rise of populist sentiment, the resurgence of authoritarian demagogues in former fascist countries and the emergence of such figures in traditionally stable parliamentary democracies and republics, the vituperative temper of the times fueled by immature if not dangerous radio and television commentators, and the increasing personalized hostility in the academy combine to make the need for public intellectuals of credibility, civility of manner, and life integrity hyper-urgent.

If this is true in the political order, it is now especially true in the ecclesial order as well. Catholic opinion is not simply divided—that is fine, after all, as Newman reminds us of the importance of Catholic intellects in collision with Catholic intellects, and not only as it applies to doctrinal definitions and moral instruction—but divided in ways that harken back to a period when mutual anathemas were flung around with righteous cruelty. Personalities are vilified with predicable assurance, exclusive claims of orthodoxy are rampant, intolerance for the larger Tradition trumped without ceasing, and organic conservatism disparaged mercilessly.

This ain't good.

The recovery of the Catholic public intellectual—an undertaking at the heart of this essay—is not a luxury, a divertissement, an obscurantist indulgence. It is a moral necessity.

If Cameron's lament over the failure of Catholic scholars to engage with the popular media had some potency in the 1970s and 1980s—the years of our academic relationship and then friendship—they have greater credibility now.

In Canada, the intellectual vibrancy to be found in Catholic circles in the twentieth century with the likes of the social thinkers Moses Coady and Jimmy Tompkins, the novelist Morley Callaghan, the educator Alphonse-Marie Parent, the sociologist Georges-Henri Lévesque, the theologian, ecumenist, and activist Gregory Baum, the editor and politician Claude Ryan, the philosopher and writer Mary Jo Leddy, the visionary communications genius Marshall McLuhan, and the philosopher prime minister Pierre Elliott Trudeau has not been rejuvenated by the next generation. Catholic publications have become as rare as church attendance in post–Quiet Revolution Quebec. And this although there are some twenty tertiary-level Catholic institutions in the country, three provinces with full funding for parochial schools from primary through secondary, and an impressive array of hospitals dotting the landscape.

There is certainly significant scholarship being done at the highest level of research and publication by Catholic scholars in Catholic universities and by Catholic scholars in secular universities, and there are Catholic leaders in every dimension of society bringing to bear in their decision-making powerful determinatives from their Catholic upbringing.

But self-identified Catholic intellectuals willing to engage in broader public discourse are infinitesimal in number. A Catholic perspective has disappeared from the public forum, either in hiding, prudentially self-restricted, or judged unfashionable, a residual memory of a time when religion defined us. Why has that voice been muted?

In the United States the climate for a clear Catholic presence, precisely as *Catholic*, hasn't been entirely soured. Self-declared Catholic columnists and commentators—some of whom wear the mantle of public Catholic intellectuals like E. J. Dionne, Garry Wills, Paul Elie, and Mary Gordon—if not ubiquitous, are at least not a distant memory. Admittedly, the zeitgeist is hardly favorable to a reprise of the Fulton Sheen era, a taste for the old apologetics—even when dressed up in Robert Barron's more media-savvy schtick—not poised for a sustained comeback.

There is a profound need for an adult-level catechesis, but that is not the same thing as leadership in the public forum providing a Catholic slant on issues—political, cultural, and philosophical—in such a mode and manner as to ensure critical respect from disparate and occasionally hostile quarters.

The audience receptive to the insights and critiques coming from Newman and Merton—and Cameron to boot—was wide, pan-Catholic, public, ecumenical, and secular. What they said mattered; they had the credibility that comes from learning and from their capacity to engage in a scrutiny of their own tradition when they found it wanting. In other words, their intellectual honesty and transparency guaranteed a respectful if not always a warm and persuaded community of listeners and readers. They knew how important it is to make a case that is firm in its inherent logic, its presuppositions on open display, its tone aggressive when necessary but never stooping to the status of an *argumentum ad auctoritatem* or an *argumentum ad hominem.*

There is a wide chasm that separates the polemicist no matter how media-crafty or publicly connected—I am thinking specifically of Richard Neuhaus, the dynamic scourge of those who did not fall under his narrow rubric of what it means to be Catholic or indeed politically free—from the expansive spirit of jolly but penetrating engagement that characterized Chesterton's witty and affective combativeness with George Bernard Shaw.

Eviscerating the Philistines is always an easy thing to do. The tang of victory is sweet. But the victory is evanescent. Superficial point-scoring has its media appeal, but the aftertaste among the interlocutors is far less satisfying—if they are honest. The dominance of talk radio and the commanding presence of loud opinion-shapers schooled in the Fox News modality, panelists prodded into clamorous intervention mode à la CNN, make it difficult to create a platform for *actual* debate—fiery but civil, driven by conviction but open to persuasion. The G. K. Chesterton–George Bernard Shaw debates were models of such clever intellectual repartee, solid positions but supple in expression, a playing to the audience that combined the entertaining with the pedagogical in sharp contrast with manipulative rabble rousing. Not sure that such a model is at all replicable in the current climate, so polarized have we become, so attached to the technologies that free us from ordinary decencies, so acclimated to a media world of incessant barking, cacophony, and lethal mayhem.

Newman and Merton were conscious of their public role, indeed often reveled in it. They were hardly milquetoasts, cowering in the corner, fearful of generating controversy. But neither were they publicity hounds, keen on maximizing coverage, fond of the calculated *frisson*, happy to whip up the ire of authority. In fact, they felt the rod of authority's displeasure more than once.

Newman had to face down his detractors at home and abroad, and so did Merton. Both, despite the success they brought their respective communities—the Oratorians and the Cistercians of the Strict Observance—encountered opposition within their ranks from those who feared their influence, resented their popularity, or simply misunderstood them.

Newman's interest in, sometimes passion for, but never indifference to, novel or conflicting ideas; his sturdy faith in the evolutionary capacity of ideas, as expressed so poetically in his *Essay on the Development of Christian Doctrine* (1845 with a subsequent 1878 edition with extensive revisions); and his abiding conviction that truth need fear nothing inspired Merton to write in two separate journal entries in 1965 of his respect for the English cardinal:

> My admiration for Newman grows constantly, the more I know the details of his life and all the nonsense he had to suffer from almost everyone and especially from the hierarchy of the church. With what good sense and patience he took it after all (May 30, 1965)....Look what the hierarchy did to him! (July 9, 1965)[1]

Censored, invigilated, delated, and instructed to desist writing on issues perceived by the Trappist establishment as unbefitting a monk, a source of scandal, the perfect picture of the rebellious son, Merton wrote in a letter to his brother Trappist, Anthony Chassagne,

> At the mere mention of censors I tend to see red...when some rather rattle-brained monks with no experience of the world, and still less of publishing, air their private fantasies about what constitutes an opportune publication, and can maintain it against the opposition of the entire publishing business, plus eminent and even intelligent persons of the laity and the hierarchy....Oh well. Years ago you recommended that I get to know Newman, and I did

> not see your point. I certainly do now, not that I can compare my griefs with his in this matter of censorship.[2]

But it wasn't only in the area of censorship that Merton found a kinship with Newman. They had struggles with members of their own community—Frederick Faber with Newman, and Merton with his abbot, James Fox—and they had fellow Catholics who queried their ecclesial fidelity, questioned the direction of their writing and intellectual probing, and deplored the effect they were having on subsequent generations of English converts in the case of Newman and junior monks in the case of Merton.

In Merton's eyes, Newman was quintessentially English and monastic in temperament and inclination, rejecting the revivified but ultimately ineffectual baroque theology of Henry Edward Manning and Wilfrid Ward and the antiquated medievalism of Augustus Welby Pugin and the Anglo-Catholic Ritualists. By contrast, Merton situates Newman, and coincidently himself, firmly in the ancient and patristic tradition:

> Cardinal Newman was too Catholic to be anything but an English Catholic. His Catholic instinct told him that universality did not demand renunciation of his English outlook

> and spiritual heritage. Hence, he did not follow the more romantic converts of his time. Or rather, though he was momentarily influenced by them, it was just long enough to discover with alarm that he could be untrue to himself and to his authentic sense of the English tradition. Having once wavered in the presence of the overcompensation practiced by some of his colleagues, for whom nothing was sufficiently un-English, or too aggressively Roman, he drew back in salutary fear from the abyss of exotic and baroque clichés into which he saw himself about to fall headlong. He preserved the simplicity of his English devotion, and the clarity of the English spiritual idiom.[3]

Whether withstanding a barrage of criticism from his fellow and deeply distrusting Roman Catholics, generating controversy nationwide with his essays, commentaries, and books, coping with his devoted Oratorian brothers engaged in civil war (the bad feeling between the Brompton Oratory in London and the Birmingham Oratory speaks sadly to the fractious and divisive atmosphere that many attributed to Newman), struggling with his abiding sense of failure over the Irish university project and the upheaval that attended on the direction of *The Rambler*, Newman's faith was a bulwark, his affective spirituality a still point in the whirligig of his life.

Merton admired that spiritual sturdiness, that intellectual fortitude he discovered in Newman, and he came in his later life to feel close to a figure he once intentionally kept his distance from:

> There are people one meets in books or in life whom one does not merely observe, meet, or know. A deep resonance of one's entire being is immediately set up with the entire being of the other (*Cor ad cor loquitur*)—heart speaks to heart in the wholeness of the language of music; true friendship is a kind of singing. Yet for a long time I had no "resonance" with Newman (because I did not bother to listen for any; I think pictures of him scared me). I was suspicious of letting him in....But now I want all the music...and am with difficulty restrained from taking too many books of Newman out of the library when I have more books than I need already.[4]

Merton's love of Newman, similar to my own, is built on his sturdy defense of the Catholic Tradition devoid of malice toward his adversaries, intellectual and personal; his elegance of style, treasuring the word through sensitive deployment rather than harnessing it to fiery polemic; his contemplative disposition; his refined literary sensibility; and his devotion to truth—a truth grasped through dialogue and tension, through his celebrated collision of Catholic intellects.

For Newman, the purpose of theology itself is not to police, to regurgitate, to serve as authority's willing handmaiden, but to engage in the exalted task of shaping the church's self-understanding, of preparing the church for change, in fact, "accustoming the mind of Catholics to the idea of change."

The Catholic genius is truly comprehensive and inclined not to exclude but to incorporate, to seek the perfect synthesis, and it is the function of theology, in Newman's mind, given that theology is the "regulating principle" of its life, to articulate that synthesis.

But always the efforts of the theologian must flow from that obedience to conscience that serves as *the* definitive guide in his or her life, indeed in the life of all persons of goodwill. Newman knew from personal experience the exacting costs demanded by conscience. It propelled him to leave what he knew and loved to embrace what was foreign and not a little frightening. His careful reading of the church fathers and the controversies that marked the early centuries of the emerging church compelled him in the end to conclude that the *ecclesia anglicana*, his *via media*, was not insulated from heresy or error. And so began the slow trip from the Thames to the Tiber.

Of the power and role of conscience Newman was to write much over the years, but the most extended and well-known treatment can be found in *A Letter Addressed to the Duke of Norfolk on Occasion of Mr. Gladstone's Recent Expostulation*. An embittered prime minster, William Gladstone (a politician deeply knowledgeable about matters ecclesiastical)—smarting from his electoral defeat in 1874, which he attributed to the influence of the Irish Catholic hierarchy over Catholic Members of Parliament—penned his provocative pamphlet *The Vatican Decrees in Their Bearing on Civil Allegiance: A Political Expostulation* (Victorians had a penchant for lengthy titles) in which he concluded that after the dogmatic definition of papal infallibility in 1870, Catholics could, *ipso facto*, no longer be considered loyal citizens of the state. The reputation of all English Catholics was impugned, as the credibility of all Roman clergy had been called into question by Kingsley, resulting in the *Apologia*. The new rejoinder: *A Letter to Norfolk*.

As part of his argument, demonstrating that English Catholics can be loyal to both the crown and the pope, Newman appealed directly to conscience:

> When Anglicans, Wesleyans, the various Presbyterian sects in Scotland, and other denominations

> among us, speak of conscience, they mean what we mean, the voice of God in the nature and heart of man....They speak of a principle planted within us, before we have had any training....They consider it a constituent element of the mind, as our perception of other ideas may be, as our powers of reasoning, as our sense of order and the beautiful, and our other intellectual endowments. They consider it, as Catholics consider it, to be the internal witness of both the existence and the law of God.... Conscience is the aboriginal Vicar of Christ, a prophet in its informations, a monarch in its peremptoriness, a priest in its blessings and anathemas.[5]

Newman is clear on the supreme authority of conscience as he refers to the Fourth Lateran Council of 1216 and its dictum that they who act against conscience lose their souls. Newman concluded his section on conscience in his *Letter to Norfolk* with his brilliant and oft-quoted peroration: "Certainly, if I am obliged to bring religion into after dinner toasts (which indeed does not seem quite the thing) I shall drink—to the Pope, if you please,—still, to Conscience first, and to the Pope afterwards."[6]

The teaching of Newman on conscience has been influential both during the Second Vatican Council and during the tumultuous period immediately following the publication of Pope Paul VI's encyclical on upholding the ban against all forms of artificial birth regulation, *Humanae vitae* in 1968.

Cameron saw in Newman's teaching on conscience an intellectual and spiritual response to the turmoil created by the encyclical, and years later, while teaching at St. Jerome's University in the University of Waterloo, I undertook the task as official co-biographer of Canada's preeminent Anglophone Catholic church leader, Gerald Emmett Cardinal Carter to explore Newman's thinking on conscience in a particularly arresting way. At the time of writing the biography, Carter was the archbishop of Toronto, an internationally recognized expert on catechetics, an astute churchman often more comfortable in board rooms and political chambers than in a sanctuary, impressively well read, a bilingual, and an adviser to popes on financial matters. He was the uncontested leader of the Catholic Church in the country.

But he earned his chops long before his appointment to Toronto and his subsequent creation as a cardinal. He established his reputation as a major figure shaping the response of the Canadian bishops to the crisis of faith engendered by *Humanae vitae*.

The Canadian bishops had issued a document at the time of the encyclical, what became known as the Winnipeg Statement,[7] a document not unlike that of other episcopal conferences throughout the world that responded to the shock and dismay of countless numbers of Catholics—and non-Catholics as well—who anticipated, and in some instances were led to believe, that the teaching of the church on birth control would change. That was not the case. Rather than simply reiterate the Roman magisterium's ban, they sought a pastoral approach that would take into consideration the needs of laypeople and the concerns of struggling priests. The result was a skillful navigation between the shoals of the magisterium and dissenting theologians and laity. Newman's spirit can be found permeating the Statement:

> We stand in union with the Bishop of Rome.... But this very union postulates such a love of the Church that we can do no less than to place all our love and all of our intelligence at its service. If this sometimes means that in our desire to make the Church more intelligible and more beautiful we must, as pilgrims do, falter in the way or differ as to the way, no one should conclude that our common faith is lost or our loving purpose blunted. The great Cardinal Newman once wrote: *lead kindly light amidst the encircling gloom.* We believe that the Kindly Light will lead us to a greater understanding of the ways of God and the love of men.[8]

Carter was a major shaper behind the scenes of the Winnipeg Statement, and when some confusion prompted the need, as he saw it, for a clarification of the statement in light of strong criticism of the Canadian hierarchy as disloyal to the pope, he issued his own clarification, which he dutifully ran past his brothers in the episcopate.

But the problem wouldn't go away. So the Canadian bishops published their "Statement on the Formation of Conscience" in 1973. Carter was the document's midwife. It was a well-reasoned, if somewhat dry, examination of the various types of conscience as well as the processes involved in the formation of a mature conscience. Its references to Scripture are bountiful, and it contains ample allusions to the church fathers and conciliar documents. It is a careful and intelligent work. Neither confrontational in tone nor timid in argument for a "dynamic Christian conscience," Carter remained an adroit centrist, even if his theological sympathies were liberal. He always had his eye on Rome.

The governing spirit of the conscience document is Newman. Discernment, reflection, sensitive listening, and informed spiritual judgment are the stuff of a mature conscience, and the magisterium has its role to play, but the Newman of the *Letter to Norfolk* and *Consulting the Faithful in Matters of Doctrine* is embedded in the text.

Newman, too, always had his eye on Rome because Rome had its eye on him. If Carter's attentiveness to Rome was predicated in part on his ecclesiastical careerism, for Newman it was the result of his painful knowledge that Rome viewed him as a problem.

The primacy of conscience for Newman was not to be conceived as a license for latitudinarian sympathies. He was not partial to diminishing the power of legitimate religious authority or of compromising the "dogmatic principle," the one remaining bulwark, as he saw it, against the ravages of liberalism. Conscience is no more whim for Newman than religion is sentiment.

Cameron valued the satirist in Newman and allowed that the novel was his principal métier when exercising his gift for humor and parody and when skewering the pompous and misguided. And so, I diligently read *Loss and Gain: The Story of a Convert* and *Callista: A Sketch of the Third Century*, Newman's two novels—he topped Merton who published only one, *My Argument with the Gestapo*—and although neither sits high on the list of Victorian novels of genius, each speaks directly to Newman's disdain for credulousness and soppy enthusiasm.

In *Loss and Gain*, Newman's fictional protagonist Charles Reding, a young Oxford student and soon-to-be Roman convert, suffers a visitation of proselytizing representatives from the broadest spectrum of British religious life, one of whom embodies the doctrinal free-for-all that Newman deplored. The young woman, who is an advocate for a new religious body and whose earnestness knows few limits, tells Reding that she and her group of ardent followers are "all for a pure religion." They are "all scriptural," each supporting some aspect of religion—most of which on the surface are in sharp contradiction—"thirsting after the river of life, whatever their personal views."

In Newman's mind this is theological mush, a pot-pourri of diverse views of various levels of rational and affective credibility, all reduced to a catholicity of view, a liberalism of sentiment, so madly eclectic and indulgent that dogma is reduced to passing convention and tradition understood as a matter of *spontaneous* invention. In contrast, Newman's tribute to conscience is not a celebration of such individualist instincts; he is not partial, as you can see, to religious indifferentism. His own search for the light, for truth, for the *real*, was a search that often proved a *via dolorosa*, a way marked by hard decisions, dark nights of misunderstanding and misperception, warring ideas and tumultuous emotions, an agony and an ecstasy. The teacher in him would not abide the easy evasions and palatable half-truths that could soothe his restive mind. The teacher in him would not tolerate anything less than the searing light.

For these reasons Newman would delight in deflating the pompous, in satirizing the sophist, in pillorying the pseudo-philosopher skilled at rhetoric but empty withal. In *Callista*, he provides us, in the person of the "great Polemo of Rhodes, the friend of Plotinus, the pupil of Theagenes, the disciple of Thrasyllus, the hearer of Nicomachus, who was of the school of Secundus, the doctor of the new Pythagoreans," a type of all those pretentious sages that the master satirist loves to excoriate.

The Bottomless, as he is known, pontificates on the obvious, engages in circular arguments that have the patina of profundity, and is carried back and forth to his chair in the lecture hall by a gaggle of adorers. Newman, the teacher—and he was always the teacher, the doctor—would have no truck with such cant, philistinism, and shallow thinking masquerading as insight. He mocks mercilessly.

As did Cameron in his various published essays and in his reviews for the *New York Review of Books*. Although Newman and Cameron demolished the academic pomposities prominent in their world, the shifting orthodoxies that shackle independent thinking, the politically correct posturing that diminishes meaningful debate, they inclined more to gentle satire than to the radical Swiftian fury preferred by Merton in his *Original Child Bomb: Points for Meditation Scratched on the Walls of a Cave* (about the atomic bomb that devastated Hiroshima) and "Chant to Be Used in Processions around a Site with Furnaces" (a visceral pillorying of the reasoning provided by a concentration camp commander when justifying the extermination of his prisoners).

A Catholic public intellectual for our time modeled on the performative witness and integrity of faith in the life, spirituality, and thought of John Henry Newman is more than an attractive proposition. It is, in my view, an urgent necessity.

My appropriation of Newman was facilitated in great measure by my study *under* James M. Cameron and my study *of* Thomas Merton, both intelligent interpreters of Newman and inspiring figures in their own right.

But the larger appeal of Newman—outside the world of the professional Victorianist, the historical theologian, claimants of the Newman legacy on both the ecclesiastical left and right—rests on his rise to greater heights of visibility through his canonization.

The politics of canonization is a fascinating area of study and the reasons behind the cause for Newman's sainthood, the timing, curial intrigues, motivations around advocacy, determinations of "heroicity of virtue," confirmation by the medical consulta of the required miracle at the beatification or penultimate stage followed by the requisite miracle necessary prior to approval by the pontiff for canonization, these are all necessary steps on the ladder to the sacred empyrean. Does it really matter when making the case that Newman is an ideal exemplar of the Catholic intellectual by having him included among the "cloud of witnesses"?

It does, I believe, because, as I have argued elsewhere,

> in our postmodern, globalized world, we hunger even more than ever for communion, for connectedness, and in the ancient teaching on saints we can discover anew an antidote to the widespread feeling of existential loneliness, of cosmic isolation, that seems such an acute feature of our time. Sainthood as pap, as easy medicine for the frightened specks who inhabit the universe is not quite what I have in mind. The saints are not fodder for the superstitious, nor commodities for those entrepreneurs with an eye for marketing to the devout....The saints have given themselves over to that "mystery, that perplexity and frustration" that we call God, and because they are the true stalkers of the holy, they speak to our collective need for transhistorical meaning, for perpetuity, to be "alone with the Alone." The saints are not an antidote to our agnosticism. They are a still point in the whirligig that is life, an aperture to wholeness.[9]

Newman, then, as a model of light, serenity, and sanity in our dark and polarized time is especially suited for those who would harness their intellectual interests and specializations for the benefit of humankind, sifting their expertise and faith through the lens of confident yet humble Catholicism—neither restorationist nor recidivist. Just ever-regenerating, ever-revivifying.

NOTES

PREFACE

1. Eamon Duffy, *John Henry Newman: A Very Brief History* (London: SPCK, 2019), 2.

I. MY JOURNEY WITH NEWMAN

1. James M. Cameron, *On the Idea of a University* (Toronto: University of Toronto Press, 1978), 49.

2. Charles Stephen Dessain, *John Henry Newman* (London: Adam & Charles Black, 1971), 168–69.

3. As quoted in Michael W. Higgins, "John Henry Newman: A Century of Influence," *Grail: An Ecumenical Journal* 7, no. 3 (September 1991): 46–47.

II. "WHO ARE THE LAITY?"

1. Ian Ker, *John Henry Newman: A Biography* (Oxford: Oxford University Press, 1989), viii.

2. John Henry Newman, *On Consulting the Faithful in Matters of Doctrine*, ed. John Coulson (London: Collins, 1986), 17–18.

3. Coulson, "Introduction," in Newman, *On Consulting the Faithful in Matters of Doctrine*, 41.

4. "Glimpses of Newman," drawn from *Discussions and Arguments* and *A Grammar of Assent*, *The Tablet* 12 (October 2019): 5.

5. Newman, *On Consulting the Faithful in Matters of Doctrine*, 55.

6. Newman, *On Consulting the Faithful in Matters of Doctrine*, 63.

7. Newman, *On Consulting the Faithful in Matters of Doctrine*, 106.

III. NEWMAN, MODEL FOR CONTEMPORARY CATHOLIC INTELLECTUALS

1. As quoted in Ian Ker, *John Henry Newman: A Biography* (Oxford: Oxford University Press, 1989), 433–44; italics mine.

2. As quoted in Ker, *John Henry Newman: A Biography*, 410.

3. John Henry Newman, *Discourses on the Scope and Nature of University Education Addressed to the Catholics of Dublin* (London: Dent, 1965), 101.

4. Henri J. M. Nouwen, *Lifesigns: Intimacy, Fecundity, and Ecstasy in Christian Perspective* (New York: Image Books/Doubleday, 1986), 49–50.

5. Newman, *Discourses on the Scope and Nature of University Education*, 129–30.

6. Newman, *Discourses on the Scope and Nature of University Education*, 122.

IV. NEWMAN TODAY

1. Bernard Lonergan, *Collected Works of Bernard Lonergan*, vol. 4 (Toronto: University of Toronto Press, 1993), 238.

2. Roderick Strange, *John Henry Newman: A Portrait in Letters* (Oxford: Oxford University Press, 2015), 431–32.

3. Michael W. Higgins, "From the Monkish Scribe to the Digital Age: The University Both Continuous and Transformed," in *Universities at Risk: How Politics, Special Interests and Corporatization Threaten Academic Integrity* (Toronto: James Lorimer and Company, 2008), 291.

4. Donald Nicholl, *The Beatitude of Truth: Reflections of a Lifetime* (London: Darton, Longman & Todd, 1997), 5–6.

V. NEWMAN, MERTON, AND THE RETURN TO THE SOURCES

1. Thomas Merton, *The Sign of Jonas* (New York: Doubleday/Image, 1956), 57.

2. Thomas Merton, *Conjectures of a Guilty Bystander* (New York: Doubleday/Image, 1968), 24–25.

3. Thomas Merton, *Clement of Alexandria: Selections from the Protreptikos* (New York: New Directions, 1962), 5–6.

4. Ian Ker, *John Henry Newman: A Biography* (Oxford: Oxford University Press, 1989), 583, quoting from Newman's *Certain Difficulties Felt by Anglicans in Catholic Teaching*, vol. 2.

5. Ker, *John Henry Newman: A Biography*, 522–23, quoting from *The Letters and Diaries of John Henry Newman*, vol. 20; italics mine.

6. John Henry Newman, *Apologia pro Vita Sua*, ed. Martin J. Svaglic (Oxford: Oxford University Press, 1967), 224–26.

VI. THE CONTINUING RELEVANCE OF NEWMAN

1. Thomas Merton, *A Vow of Conversation: Journals 1964–1965* (New York: Farrar Straus Giroux, 1988), 186, 199.

2. Thomas Merton, *The School of Charity: The Letters of Thomas Merton on Religious Renewal and Spiritual Direction*, ed. Brother Patrick Hart, OCSO (New York: Farrar Straus Giroux, 1990), 181.

3. Thomas Merton, "The English Mystics," in *Mystics and Zen Masters* (New York: Delta, 1967), 129.

4. Thomas Merton, *Conjectures of a Guilty Bystander* (New York: Doubleday/Image, 1968), 188.

5. John Henry Newman, *A Letter Addressed to the Duke of Norfolk on Occasion of Mr. Gladstone's Recent Expostulation* (London: Aeterna Press, 2015), 42.

6. Newman, *A Letter to the Duke of Norfolk*, 50.

7. The Winnipeg Statement was a document issued by the Canadian Bishops' Conference in September 1968, in response to Paul VI's encyclical *Humanae vitae*. It affirmed their solidarity with the pope while at the same time expressing pastoral concern for the needs of the faithful and their exercise of conscience.

8. As quoted in Michael W. Higgins and Douglas R. Letson, *My Father's Business: A Biography of His Eminence G. Emmett Cardinal Carter* (Toronto: Macmillan, 1990), 108.

9. Michael W. Higgins, *Stalking the Holy: The Pursuit of Saint Making* (Toronto: Anansi, 2006), 17, 25.